MEGHAN HERTZFELDT
ILLUSTRATIONS BY LINDSAY LEAL

Game Time: Alex and the Big Assist

Copyright ©2023 Meghan Hertzfeldt

All rights reserved. No part of this publication may be reproduced, distributed, or transmitted in any form or by any means, including photocopying, recording, or other electronic or mechanical methods, without the prior written permission of the publisher, except in case of brief quotations embodied in critical reviews and certain other noncommercial uses permitted by copyright law.

ISBN: 978-1-960111-08-1

Library of Congress Control Number: 2023906354

Names, characters, and places are products of the author's imagination. Front cover image, illustrations, and book design by Lindsay Leal. First printing edition 2023.

Published by Rodney K Press
www.rodneykpress.com

*To Max and John...
Don't forget to air out your hockey gear.
It stinks.*

—

In loving memory of Tim Hertzfeldt, a true Wisconsin hockey dad, who dedicated many early mornings at the rink.

CHAPTER 1

THE PREGAME

"OUCH!" ALEX YELPED. He jumped out of bed, holding onto his lip. He looked at his hands and checked for blood. Nothing. He must have dozed off and dreamt about getting a high stick to his face. Alex took a deep breath. *Good thing that was just a dream,* he thought to himself.

Alex stretched as he looked around his new bedroom filled with moving boxes. His elbow knocked the corner of a box. It fell to the floor and was tipped on its side. The label on it read,

"Dad's office." A small black object slowly rolled out of the box he had just knocked over. That's when he saw it."

No way! It can't be, he thought to himself. His eyes grew wide. It was his dad's favorite collectible, a puck from Game 7 of the 1993 Stanley Cup Playoffs. That box definitely shouldn't have been in his new bedroom.

Alex knew this puck meant the world to his dad. It was also very valuable, so he knew he shouldn't touch it. He shouldn't even go near it! That thing was worth so much money it was priceless! But . . . Alex loved hockey. He was possibly the biggest fan of hockey that ever was. He just wanted to get a closer look.

"Don't do it, Alex," he said to himself. "This isn't gonna end well!" He rubbed his sweaty palms together and inched a little closer to the puck. "This is Dad's favorite thing. This is off-limits. It's like lava. It's—"

Alex froze.

Just as his fingertips touched the puck, his bedroom door burst open. He jumped back, hitting his other arm on the foot of his bed.

"Gah! Don't you know how to knock?" He stared at the tiny boy in the doorway who held a little red blanket. "You scared me! Aren't you supposed to be napping or doing what babies do?"

"Nappy, nappy, me no take nappy." Connor, his little brother, broke into a fit of giggles.

Alex rolled his eyes and quickly stepped toward his brother. He tugged on the little red blanket. Connor stumbled into his room.

"Shhh," Alex said with his finger on

his lips. "Look, I'll play with you in a few minutes, I promise. Right now, I need you to go downstairs and act like you need a snack. Can you do that for your favorite big brother?"

"Me no nappy. Me happy! Me wanna play with brother! Vrooooom!" Connor said. "Connor wanna play cars!"

"Listen, Connor, I'll make you a deal. You go ask mom for an applesauce pouch and I promise I'll play monster trucks before dinner. Okay?" Alex asked.

Connor looked hurt. He was sad Alex couldn't play right then and there. Then slowly, a smile spread across his face when he realized he had to go get a snack. He loved snacks. He grabbed his red blanket and headed down the stairs toward their new kitchen. Alex knew his brother loved to play cars. This deal might have given him a few minutes.

Alex grabbed his door handle and slowly pushed it shut. Once the bedroom door clicked, Alex glanced at the puck again. This time, he marched to it and picked it up. He slowly lifted it to his brown eyes. He was amazed to read the words, "Stanley Cup Playoffs." The puck also had the Los Angeles Kings logo. Alex knew this was a very special puck.

A knot formed in Alex's throat. Alex and his family had just moved to Colorado from Wisconsin. He thought about all the memories he had of his friends. They had played on a hockey team together. They loved to watch hockey together, too. Alex loved playing outdoor hockey at the pond close to his old house. Remembering the fun times with his buddies made him miss home . . . or what home used to be.

Alex walked to his bedroom window, still holding the puck. He could see the Rocky Mountains from his room. He looked across the street at the unfamiliar houses.

He wondered, *Are there any kids who live on my street? Will any of them want to play with me? Will they go to my school?*

He took a deep breath and thought about the new friends he wanted to make.

"Alex! Are you up here?" His mom's voice broke his thoughts. "Oh, there you are, honey!" his mom said as she walked into his room. "Connor came down and said you wanted an applesauce pouch. We don't have any because I haven't been to the store yet—"

His mom stopped talking when she saw what he was holding.

"Is that what I think it is? Dad's puck

from his office?" she asked. She glanced at the puck in Alex's hand and back up to his face.

She looked around the room. She picked up the box from the floor and saw the label "Dad's office." Alex gulped.

"I knocked over the box and the puck fell out. I wasn't snooping, I . . . I . . . I promise," Alex stuttered.

"Why don't you let me take this," she said as she gently took the puck from Alex's hand. "I'll put it in Dad's office while you get ready for dinner, okay?" She picked up the box and set it on her hip. "Monday is a big day! You start third grade at your new school. Are you excited?"

"Uh, yeah," Alex replied, staring back out the window across the street.

"Oh, I was able to get the cable set up today. I'll let you watch some of the

Avalanche game before bed. It's not every day you move to the state where your favorite hockey team plays," she said with a wink.

"Thanks, Mom. I'll be down in a bit," he replied. He glanced anxiously around the bare cream-colored walls of his room.

Sensing something was wrong, his mom placed her hand on his shoulder. "You know, you can video chat with your friends back home. And you will get to see them this summer when we go back to visit. Just think of all the nice kids you're going to meet once you go to school and start playing hockey. You can never have too many friends."

"Yeah, I guess," Alex said, shrugging his shoulders.

Alex waited for his mom to close the door. Before he got ready for dinner, he needed to find something—the one thing that would make his new room feel like home. The rest of the boxes could wait to be unpacked. This one could not.

"Come on," he mumbled to himself. "Where is it?" He frantically moved the boxes one at a time. He scanned the labels.

"Nope. Not this one." He tossed it to the side.

"Definitely not this one!" he said. A box filled with socks and pajamas tumbled to the floor.

Alex heard his mom calling up the staircase to see if he'd washed his hands.

"Almost done, Mom!" he replied as he continued the search.

"Where are you, Great One?" Alex muttered. He started moving faster now.

Alex tossed his underwear one by one as he dug through the box.

Just then, he heard a click and the doorknob turned.

"Alex, what in the world? It looks like a tornado went through here! We haven't lived in our new home for 12 hours and you've somehow managed to make your room look like it barfed up clothes!"

His mother looked around the room with disappointment. "Can I at least ask what you're looking for here? It certainly isn't a pair of underwear, as I see all of those are on your lampshade!"

"Uhhh . . . nothing," Alex responded with a slight shake in his voice.

"I told you, honey, we'll get unpacked this weekend."

"Well, it's just that I am a little nervous to start school on Monday.

I thought if I found my #99 poster, I could hang it on the wall tonight to make this all feel more like home."

He stared nervously. But his mom smiled and said, "Well, why didn't you tell me that ten minutes ago before you made this mess? It's in that box!"

Alex's mom pointed to a box in the corner.

"What? How did you know that?" he said.

"Ahh, Alex . . . moms always know their kids! Read the side of that box there," she said. She pointed to a homemade label he hadn't seen before.

Slowly he read, "Open first! Important stuff." A huge grin spread across his face. Looking up at his mom excitedly, he said, "Mom, you're a genius!"

Giving him a quick hug, she said,

"Oh hey, Alex? I came up because I thought you might need this." She tossed a roll of tape to him.

"Thanks, Mom," Alex said with a smile. Turning toward the box he thought to himself, *How did she know?* His mom gave him a quick wink and walked back downstairs.

Alex gathered the box and peeled back the tape. The four sides popped open. There it was, right on top! A poster of the greatest hockey player of all time was rolled tightly in a rubber band. It was a picture of Wayne Gretzky holding up the Stanley Cup when he played for the Edmonton Oilers.

Alex slowly unrolled the poster and grabbed the tape from the floor. He gently placed tape on the back. He looked around his new room, in his new home, in a new city, in a new state. *It's go time!* he thought to himself.

I hope the ponds out here freeze over. I've got to get back out on the ice.

He carefully placed the poster right above the foot of his bed so he could stare at it as he fell asleep.

The faint sound of the "Star-Spangled Banner" was playing on the TV downstairs in the living room. This was his cue to wash his hands as fast as possible. He wanted to make it downstairs in time to watch the puck drop. Tomorrow was his first full day of his life in Colorado. But he'd worry about that later. Tonight, he wanted to get lost in something that reminded him of home: hockey.

CHAPTER 2

THE WARM UP

ALEX SLOWLY ROLLED OVER IN BED and opened his eyes. The frost coating the frame of his window made his eyes go wide with excitement. He sat up quickly and jumped out of bed. Alex walked across his room, peered out his window, and saw the same thick frost on the windshield of his dad's car.

"No way!" Alex said as he dashed across his room. He flung the door open and ran down the stairs, skipping every other step. Alex grabbed the TV remote. "Come on, come on! Please tell me it's below 32 degrees..." He changed the channels until he found the local news.

"Mom! Mom! Get in here!" he called to her in the kitchen.

"Today's weather is only going to be a high of 29 degrees! Can we pllllllllease go over to that pond we drove by yesterday?" he begged.

"Sure thing!" she replied. "But eat your breakfast first."

Alex gobbled his food. With a full belly, Alex threw on his sweats, a hoodie, and his favorite jersey. He tossed his hockey bag into the back hatch of his mom's SUV. Alex, his mom, and his little brother drove toward the pond they had seen yesterday when they arrived in Denver.

Alex jumped up and down in his

seat because he was excited to get back on the ice.

"Hey, Connor. Wanna hear a joke?" Alex said excitedly, staring out the window.

"Alex, this better not be another one of your fart jokes," his mom said.

"Why should you never fart in an elevator?" Alex asked. Connor giggled while looking at Alex.

"It's wrong on so many levels!" he burst out laughing. His mom rolled her eyes, smiled, and kept driving.

When they got to the pond, not only was it frozen but there were about twenty kids skating around and shooting pucks.

That butterfly feeling in his stomach was back. Alex was nervous. All of a sudden, he felt like he couldn't step out of the car. He realized he was staring out the car window when his mom said,

"Earth to Alex? Are you going to get out?"

"Oh, right," he said.

He grabbed his gear out of the car. He started walking toward the pond to watch the hockey game. "These kids look older than me, Mom. What if they won't let me play?"

"Alex, you love to skate. Your skills show that. I'm sure once you get out there, you'll shine," his mom said with a nudge.

"Right," Alex nodded. He laced up his skates, threw on his helmet and gloves, and grabbed his stick. "Here goes nothing!" he mumbled.

Gliding across the ice felt good. Alex couldn't stop the grin from spreading across his face. He started to stick handle the puck back and forth, back and forth—

"Ooooof!"

He felt like he had run into a wall.

"Oh, I'm so sorry!" Alex said.

"No problem. Sorry, I should've been looking up," said an older kid in a black jersey. "Hey, I haven't seen you around here before. What school do you go to?"

"I just moved here from Wisconsin," Alex replied. "I start school at Coyote Point Elementary on Monday. Ya heard of it?"

"Heard of it? I go there!" he said. "I'm Blake," he held out his glove for a fist bump.

"Cool. I'm Alex," he said, bumping his fist back.

"What grade are you in?" Blake asked.

"Uh, third," Alex replied.

"Awesome. I am in fifth. Can you skate well?" Blake asked.

"Yeah, I was on a team back home.

I'm just waiting for tryouts because we just moved here," Alex said. He looked around nervously.

"Sweet. Some of the best pros are from Wisconsin and Minnesota. I'll bet you've got skills." Blake said with a smile.

"Eh, I mean, I can hold my own if that's what you're asking," Alex replied.

Blake smiled, knowing Alex was being humble. Then he asked, "So you want in on this game?" He pointed to the other kids passing the puck on the ice.

"Sure," Alex said excitedly. "That would be awesome."

"You're wearing a blue jersey, so you'll be on my team. All the blue and black jerseys out here are on a team," Blake pointed back and forth between him and Alex.

They both skated toward the pickup

game and Blake shouted, "Listen up! This is Alex. He just moved here from Wisconsin. He's on my team. Alex, meet the crew. Let's gooooooo!"

Feeling more prepared, Alex joined the game.

Blake passed the puck to another kid in a black jersey. That kid passed it back to Blake. Alex skated toward the goal and looked to Blake for the puck. Blake passed it to Alex. Alex kept his stick blade close to the ice and cradled the puck. He faked a pass to his left and skated past his opponent. Alex passed it back to Blake who shot it.

"GOAL!" Blake yelled and skated over to Alex for a quick fist bump.

He tapped his helmet and said, "Nice pass!" The other teammates skated over. One said, "Where did you learn to skate like that?"

"Yeah, no joke! That was insane!" said a girl as she spat out her mouthguard.

"Did you *live* on the frozen ponds in Wisconsin or what?" Blake joked to the group of kids.

"Well, that was a great pass," said the girl with the mouthguard. "Hey, Blake! Maybe you should move to Wisconsin to learn how to pass," the girl joked.

The group of kids laughed hysterically.

"Ohhhh! Blake got roasted!" said a kid in an orange jersey as he laughed at her comment.

Blake rolled his eyes. "Alex, that's my sister, Hannah. She's also in third grade."

"Hey, maybe I'll see you at school Monday. I've got to go. I've got a birthday party to get to right now. Nice to meet you, Alex," she said as she skated away.

Alex continued to play with the group

for the next few hours. As the sun started to warm the air, the ice began to get slushy, which was their cue to get off the pond.

The kids dripped with sweat as they packed up their gear. Blake called out, "Hey Alex. Nice game today. See you Monday, okay?" Alex looked up as he unlaced his skates.

"Yeah, cool. See you at school," he replied.

Alex was smiling ear to ear as he finished taking off his elbow pads and tossed his gear into his bag. *That was awesome!* he thought to himself, chugging his sports drink.

He walked back to his mom's car, piled his gear into the back, and they all headed home.

When they got home, Alex dropped his hockey bag as soon as he walked through the door. He ran upstairs and grabbed his mini hockey stick from the box he'd opened last night. Alex started taking shots against his door, thinking about the fun he'd had at the pond.

There was a sudden knock at his door. Alex's dad slowly cracked the door and poked his head inside Alex's room. His dad had heard Alex shooting pucks against the door and wanted to make sure he didn't get a puck shot at his face when he went in.

"Hey, Mom said you played at the pond today. How did it go?" his dad said as he walked into Alex's room.

"The ice was great! It felt good to skate again."

"So, who did you play with?"

"A bunch of kids. This one kid named Blake asked me to play," he replied. Alex went on to give his dad the play-by-play

of his time on the ice. After telling his dad the story, he realized that Hannah was the only kid his age. He hadn't met any other kids that might be in his class. That made him feel a little uneasy again.

"That's great. I can tell you had a blast!" said his Dad.

"Yeah, it was fun . . . " Alex smiled. But then he looked down. "It reminded me of home."

"That's a good thing, right?" his dad said.

"Yes. But I'm kind of worried about starting school on Monday," Alex said quietly.

"Moving can be nerve-wracking. But it can be exciting too. Remember when Kate, Jordy, and June moved to our street right before school ended last year?" his dad asked.

"Yes . . . " Alex replied.

"Well, they probably felt like how you feel right now. Did you know being nervous and anxious is almost an identical feeling to excitement?"

"It is?" Alex said.

"Sure is. The brain is pretty cool like that. It's okay to be nervous *and* excited," he explained. "Kids and adults go through things in life that make them feel all kinds of ways. When you take risks, you grow as a person and as a friend. Moving to a new place can do that."

"Yeah, yeah. I get it. I was a nice friend back home to our neighbors, Jordy, Kate, and June, so someone will hopefully be nice to me," Alex responded.

"All I'm saying is, be the friend you've always wanted. Just be yourself," his dad said reassuringly. "Someone wise once said, 'The day I stop learning is the day I stop growing.'"

"Who said that? The Great One?"

Alex asked, grabbing another stick from the pile in the corner of his room.

His dad took the stick from Alex and said, "You know it! Now are you going to shoot on me or what? I've been working on my blocks. My goalie skills are sick."

"Dad, it's not cool when you say 'sick!'" Alex joked.

"Yeah, sick bro, sick!" his dad said.

"Whatever, Dad!" Alex rolled his eyes. "You're goin' down!"

Alex shot the foam puck right between his legs. His dad fell backward laughing. He sat up slowly and tossed the puck back to Alex.

"Best out of three?" he asked.

CHAPTER 3

THE PUCK DROP

ALEX FELT NERVOUS AS HE WALKED up the large steps to his new school. He paused at the door. His mom nudged him forward. The bell rang, alerting students that it was time to get to class.

Alex's mom walked him to the front office. After she signed some papers she turned to Alex and said, "Good luck today. Remember, just be yourself. Everything else will fall into place."

She gave Alex a quick hug and left. A nice woman from the front office walked Alex to his new classroom.

CREEEEEK! The woman opened the old wooden door and the whole class stopped talking. All of the students were staring at the doorway in the front of the classroom, looking directly at Alex and the woman. He stood there frozen, unable to say a word. His new teacher walked over to them. The woman from the office handed a piece of paper to his new teacher.

"Hi, I'm Ms. Presley," she said, smiling as she shook his hand. Ms. Presley turned to the class. "Class, we have a new student all the way from Wisconsin. Meet Alex!" She instructed the class to gather in a circle on the rug for a quick morning meeting.

Alex slowly walked to the circle of students in the front of the classroom next to the smart board. He sat down next to a kid wearing a Broncos jersey.

Alex felt a tap on his shoulder. It was Hannah, the girl he had met at the pond.

"Hey, Alex," she said smiling. "Long time no see."

"Hey!" Alex responded, happy to see a familiar face.

"I'm Russell," said the kid in the Broncos jersey. "You got any good cheese in your lunch?"

"Huh?" Alex said.

"You're from Wisconsin, right? Isn't that like the cheese capital of the world or something?"

Hannah laughed.

"Russell, if I were you, I'd lay off the cheese. My nose can't take it anymore!"

"My farts aren't thaaaaat bad!" he rolled his eyes at Hannah.

"Hey, Russell," Hannah whispered. "Why did the chicken cross the road?"

Russell and Alex waited for the answer.

"Because the chicken sitting next to him farted!" she giggled.

"Hey, Hannah," Alex whispered back. "Why did the girl stop telling fart jokes?"

Hannah sat there, curious.

"Because everyone told her they stink!" he said.

Russel high-fived Alex. All three kids cracked up.

"Now, class, listen up . . . " Ms. Presley started the morning meeting.

Hannah pointed at Alex and said to Russell, "I think we met our match with this one. Alex, you want to sit with us at lunch?"

"Sure!" Alex said with a smile.

He thought to himself, *Maybe this move to Colorado won't be so bad after all.*

His classmates went around the

circle and introduced themselves one by one. He liked sitting next to Russell and Hannah. They made him laugh. They felt familiar, like his friends from back home.

CHAPTER 4

PERIOD ONE

THE MORNING WENT BY FAST. THE class broke out into math groups. Everyone seemed really nice. Alex played at recess with Hannah, Russell, and a few other kids from his class. It wasn't until it was time for independent reading that his day took a turn.

Sitting next to him was a really tall boy chewing gum. Well, he wasn't just chewing it—he was smacking it. He was making loud and gross sounds with his gum.

"Psst! Hey!" said the kid. He offered Alex a piece of folded paper.

Alex looked at the paper in his hand.

"Pass this over to Hannah for me," he said.

Alex shrugged his shoulders and took the piece of paper. He opened the note and read it. His eyes opened wide! The note said, "Hannah stinks at hockey and so does her gear!"

"Excuse me," said Ms. Presley. She grabbed the note out of Alex's hand. "What is this?" she asked.

Alex didn't have time to tell her that the note wasn't his. He wanted to say he didn't write it. He wanted to tell her that the tall kid had told him to pass it to Hannah.

"Alex, passing notes is not acceptable. Please meet me after class to chat."

"But I wasn't—" Alex was interrupted.

"He tried to make me pass it to Hannah, Ms. Presley," the tall kid said proudly. "But I told him that wasn't allowed." He batted his eyes at Ms. Presley.

"Thank you, Frankie," Ms. Presley said as she walked away.

Frankie smirked at Alex and pretended to read his book. Alex didn't even have a chance to tell the teacher what really happened.

When the lunch bell rang, Alex walked to his cubby. He wanted to grab his lunch from his backpack and forget about what had happened with Frankie. Hannah pulled Alex aside. "Hey, what did that note say?" she whispered.

Alex hesitated. "Uh, it was nothing really," he said looking at his feet.

"Well, steer clear of Frankie if you can," Hannah said. "He can cause trouble. The next thing you know, you'll end up getting in trouble."

Alex nodded his head.

Ms. Presley walked over to Alex. She asked, "Alex, do you have a minute?" Ms. Presley pulled him aside to chat about the note. The rest of the class was forming a line at the doorway.

Alex sat down at his desk and gulped.

Ms. Presley held the note in her hand and said, "Passing notes is not allowed during class. If I catch you again, you'll have to sit out during recess."

Alex slumped into his chair. He wasn't about to make things worse than they already were. He stood up and joined his classmates in line. They all walked to the cafeteria. Alex did not want to tell Hannah what the note said. There was no need to hurt her feelings.

CHAPTER 5

PERIOD TWO

AFTER LUNCH, MS. PRESLEY TOLD the class that they would be doing a science experiment. Alex's favorite subject was science. He hoped he would be put into a group with his new friends. He wanted to work with anyone but Frankie.

Ms. Presley posted the group names on the whiteboard.

Oh no, he thought. He felt disappointed. There it was. Frankie's name was posted right under Alex, Hannah, and Nate's names. *Now I have to work with the kid who just got me in trouble*, he thought to himself.

Ms. Presley told the kids to move into their science groups. Alex walked slowly toward his table.

The students stood around their table group. A boy named Nate with blond curly hair stood next to Alex. He handed Alex a funnel and a box of baking soda. Hannah brought the rest of the materials from the main table. Abby, a girl with large black glasses, grabbed the poster board.

"Here!" Nate said smiling. "Put these over there with the glass bottle and food coloring."

As Alex went to set the box of baking soda down, Frankie snatched it out of his hands.

"Gimme that!" Frankie said. He was

about four inches taller than Alex. Alex's jaw dropped open. He stared up at Frankie, shocked.

"Listen up. I run the show here. Alex, Abby, you hand me the materials. Nate, you can watch. Hannah, you write down what happens. I get to blow up this volcano," Frankie said, smirking.

The kids looked back and forth at each other. It was clear that everyone thought that Frankie was bossy and rude. Alex looked over at Russell's group. They were all laughing and having fun. His group wasn't sure how to respond to Frankie.

"How's it going over here?" Ms. Presley asked as she walked by.

Before the kids could speak up, Frankie said, "Great! All good over here!" He smiled at Ms. Presley. But his smile became a smirk again as soon as cience Groups:

One | Two | Three
Jenny | Sarah | Frankie
Amaya | Elliot | Nate
Steven | Jerod | Alex
Cooper | Harper | Kennedy
  | Hudson | Abby

she walked away. "Now, hand me the vinegar!" he hissed at Nate.

Frankie barked orders to the group. They did what he asked. The group wasn't sure how to stand up to him.

Alex noticed that Frankie measured the ingredients incorrectly. He wasn't even following the directions written on the board. Frankie was in a hurry to watch the volcano erupt. He didn't even have his safety goggles on. *This isn't going to end well,* Alex thought to himself.

Alex and the rest of his science group slowly stepped away from the volcano. They exchanged a few silent looks. Alex shrugged his shoulders. Nate and Abby shook their heads. The kids didn't want to get in Frankie's way *and* get yelled at.

Frankie leaned over the volcano to look inside. He added the vinegar to the

baking soda. Without warning—BAM! SPLAT!

The volcano erupted right into his face! His shirt was soaking wet. His face was covered in science lava. Frankie was so embarrassed that his face turned as red as a cherry tomato.

"This is all your fault!" Frankie yelled and pointed his finger at Alex.

Nate, Abby, Hannah, and Alex stood there staring with wide eyes and their lips tight. They were trying not to laugh at Frankie. Frankie had taken over the group and didn't listen to anything they had to say. He had skipped the steps and it literally blew up in his face.

Frankie stormed off to tell Ms. Presley. Nate whispered to the group, "How can you tell when a volcano gets angry?"

"How?" Abby whispered back.

"They blow their top!" Nate said. The whole group burst out laughing.

The kids didn't want Frankie to freak out on them so they quickly calmed down.

Nate asked, "Too soon?"

Once again, Ms. Presley asked to speak to Alex after school.

CHAPTER 6

PERIOD THREE

THERE WAS ONLY ONE WAY ALEX knew how to turn around a bad day: skate. Back in Wisconsin, Alex always played hockey after school. It was where he hung out with his best friends. The ice was where Alex felt at home.

When he skated, he didn't feel frustrated. He wasn't mad. He felt calm.

Alex went to the pond after school. He wanted to shoot pucks with Hannah and Blake before it got dark. Alex spotted Hannah and Blake laughing and joined them. He started to unzip his hockey bag to grab his gear.

"EWWWWW!" Hannah gasped. She pretended to gag.

"Bro, did you forget to air out your hockey gear?" Blake said.

"Um, yeah, I was in a hurry the other day," he said. "Whoops."

Hockey players know that if you forget to air out your gear after you're done playing, you're in for a rude awakening the next time you open your bag. It reeks!

"Hey, Alex, how do you know a clown farted?" Hannah asked.

Alex grinned at her.

"It smelled funny!" she said giggling. "Get it?"

"Yeah, yeah. Very funny." Alex smiled and rolled his eyes at her.

"So, how's it going with Frankie the Fartknocker?" Hannah asked. "He was acting like Captain Bossypants in science today."

"Yeah, bossypants is one word I'd use to describe him," he said. "He treated the group like we didn't know what we were doing." Alex shrugged his shoulders. He took a deep breath and tied his skates.

Blake said, "If it makes you feel any better, his older brother Bobby used to do the same stuff to me."

"Really?" Alex looked up.

"Yeah..." Blake paused, "until I finally stood up for myself." Blake started grinning from ear to ear.

"Oh no," said Alex. "What did you do? I have a funny feeling about this."

"Let's just say that Bobby the Bully doesn't bother Blake anymore," Hannah said smiling.

"Nah, it's not that bad," Blake said. "Bobby always tried to make fun of me for wearing glasses. He would call me names and try to knock them off my face when I'd line up for recess," he said.

Hannah and Alex stood on the ice listening.

"I would ignore Bobby and pretend I didn't hear him. That made him more upset, but eventually he left me alone. Then one day at lunch, I saw him walking toward a little boy who was also wearing glasses. I didn't want the little boy to get teased like me, so I walked right toward them with my tray of spaghetti. I stood up tall. I was nervous, but he didn't need to know that. Just as I got to Bobby to tell him to leave the boy alone, I tripped and my plate of spaghetti went right into his face!"

Hannah stood there smiling while Alex's jaw dropped.

Blake continued, "I gasped and said, 'Ohmigosh. I am so sorry! I didn't SEE you there.' Then I winked at the little boy and went to get napkins to start cleaning up my mess."

Alex looked stunned.

"From that day on, Bobby the Bully left me alone," Blake said. He tossed a few pucks out of his bag.

"So, are you saying I need to throw my lunch in Frankie's face?" Alex asked.

They started skating and passing the puck to each other.

"No. I'm definitely not saying that . . . that part was honestly an accident. What I AM saying is that he's picking on you because he's looking for attention. He is trying to make himself feel big and make you feel small. He wants to feel important," Blake said.

"So, you want me to make Frankie look small?" Alex asked.

Blake laughed and said, "No, it's not about making people feel small. It's about making the people around you stand taller."

Alex started stick-handling the puck. Tap, tap, tap, and pass. He passed the puck to Hannah. She started skating toward the net. Alex glided in a giant circle around the pond to warm up his legs. He pushed out hard on the ice and picked up speed. Alex pumped his arms and drove his skates into the ice. He crossed his right foot over his left foot and repeated the move until he started to sweat.

Alex was in the zone. He felt like he was home. He forgot about Frankie. He forgot about missing his friends. Alex started to realize right there on the pond that he was with new friends who

had his back too. A smile formed on Alex's face.

Alex was excited to video chat with his friends back home. For the first time since he moved to Colorado last weekend, he wasn't counting down the days until he could go back to Wisconsin and visit.

—

This time when he got home, Alex remembered to air out his hockey gear. There was no way he was going to wear a stinky jersey at tryouts. He ate dinner and asked his mom if it was okay to video chat with his best friend from home.

The app rang twice. Then a familiar face popped up on the screen.

"Yo!" said Will, his best friend from back home.

"Yo!" Alex said back. "You look cold!"

"I just got back from practice. Check this out." Will turned his head sideways.

"Oh no you diiiidn't! You went for the mullet!" Alex said laughing.

"Yeah! You like it?" Will asked, hoping Alex would like his new haircut. "It's all business in the front and a party in the back," Will said, pointing at the short cut at his forehead and then at the long piece behind his neck.

"Love it!" Alex said laughing. "That's some serious flow!"

"My mom said I could keep it this way through the playoffs," Will said. "If the pros grow playoff beards, then I will grow my mullet."

"You're funny. You know that?" Alex replied.

"So, how's school and stuff? Have you met anyone cooler than me yet?" Will joked.

"Nobody is as cool as you, obviously,"

he said. "But I did meet a few friends at the pond who go to my school. Hannah and Blake are brother and sister. They both play hockey and we hang at the pond. You'd love them. Hannah is super funny and Blake is a beast on the ice."

At first, Alex made it seem like everything was great—like Frankie didn't exist. But then he remembered the note in class. He remembered the science experiment. He remembered having to talk to Ms. Presley after class. After being quiet for a moment too long he heard . . .

"Alright, spill it, Flash!" Will only used his nickname when he was on the ice. Alex knew that Will could tell that something was wrong.

"Most of the kids are cool," he said. He slowly looked up at the screen. "But there is this one kid. He is driving me nuts. He keeps getting me into trouble. The worst part is, there is a rumor he's trying out for the team this weekend. It's already bad enough that he bugs me at school. The ice is the only place I can be left alone. What if we are stuck on the same team?"

"Alex. You know what Coach used to say . . . " Will said.

There was a three-second pause. Both boys said in unison, "Chins up, sticks down!"

They both smiled and laughed for a moment, remembering how Coach always said that right before they left the locker room. Then Alex grew more serious.

"We'll see," Alex said before changing the subject. "Hey, my dad's calling me into the kitchen to help with the dishes. Call me after your game this weekend and let me know how many times you score."

"You know it!" Will said. "Good luck at tryouts, Flash. Hope you don't leave too many kids in the dust."

Alex pushed the red button and ended the call. As he walked downstairs to the kitchen, he thought to himself, *When I step on the ice, everything disappears and nothing else matters*. He hoped the butterflies in his stomach would also disappear.

CHAPTER 7

OVERTIME

"TODAY WE ARE DOING THE EGG DROP Challenge," Ms. Presley said to the class. "This is going to test how well you can work as a group."

"Oh, great," Sammy said. He walked over to Alex's desk. "Just what we need. How to be a team player when your teammate does everything." He rolled his eyes and looked at Frankie's desk.

"Please grab your materials," Ms. Presley said. "Then move to your table group."

The kids all gathered their materials. They moved to their table groups and read the instructions. They needed to drop an egg from a six-foot ladder without breaking it. They started brainstorming ideas as a group.

"Why don't we use my sweatshirt?" Hannah said excitedly. "That way, when it lands, it will be safe in my hoodie."

"Why don't we wrap the egg in packing bubbles," said Abby. "I once saw a viral video where—"

"That's the worst idea ever," Frankie barked. He took the egg out of Abby's hand.

She stood there silently. Abby slowly turned a shade of bright red. She wasn't sure what to say next.

Alex decided to step in. He was annoyed and frustrated at how Frankie was treating the group. *Enough is enough!*

he thought to himself. *I've got to put an end to this madness.*

Alex stood up tall and looked Frankie right in the eyes. He could feel his hands shaking slightly and hoped nobody would catch that he was nervous.

Alex walked over to Frankie and stopped right in front of him.

"Let's let Abby finish telling us her idea," he said confidently. He pulled his shoulders back and stuck his chin out to face Frankie head on.

Frankie looked shocked. Nobody had ever stood up to him before. Frankie stood still, holding the egg in silence.

"We'd love to hear about your packing bubbles idea, Abby," Alex said.

Alex gently took the egg out of Frankie's hand and walked it back to Abby. He placed it gently in her hand. Alex smiled and winked.

The entire group was frozen. They stood still with huge smiles on their faces. Abby cleared her throat.

"As I was saying . . ." she began.

The group nodded their heads in agreement as Abby explained her idea. The other kids added their ideas as well. Well, everyone but Frankie. He stood there with his arms crossed. He was annoyed at the group. He felt jealous that everyone in the group listened to Alex and not him.

"You're so good at this," Sammy said to Alex. "You know, helping us work as a team and actually getting this project done." He passed the tape to Hannah.

"Yeah, where did you learn to do that?" Hannah winked at Alex. She could tell that he was a leader not only in the classroom but also on the ice.

"I mean . . . I guess at the hockey

rink," Alex said. "When you skate, you learn real quick how to stick up for yourself and work as a team."

Alex smiled at Hannah. She was a hockey player. She understood.

"When you are on the ice," he continued, "you have to have each other's back. You also have to set your teammates up to score. It can't always be about you, ya know?"

The kids nodded their heads and listened.

"Some of the greatest players of all time weren't the highest scorers. They were great because they passed the puck to their teammates."

After deciding on a strategy, the group started on the Egg Drop Challenge. They worked together as a team. Every member of the group had a job and played a part in their success–just like hockey.

"I want to come watch you play sometime," Sammy said to Alex.

"That reminds me," Hannah said. "Are you ready for tryouts this weekend?"

"Ready as I'll ever be," Alex said.

As it turned out, the bubble wrap idea didn't quite hold up. Just as Sammy dropped the group's egg, Frankie walked underneath the ladder. The egg fell out of the bubble wrap and SPLAT! The egg cracked over Frankie's head. The egg yolk went everywhere!

"You're gonna pay for this, Alex!" Frankie hissed, pointing his finger at Alex. He was already mad that the group didn't let him be in charge, but this made him furious.

"Oh yeah?" Alex asked. "How much?" He started pulling his lunch money out of his front pocket. "Let's see. I have $2.50. Will that do?"

The group broke out into a fit of

laughter. Frankie's face turned bright red. He was angry and stormed off to tattle once again to Ms. Presley.

CHAPTER 8

DOUBLE OVERTIME

THE BIG DAY WAS FINALLY HERE. Alex was so excited that he didn't sleep much the night before. He got to the rink and jerked the door open.

Alex walked into the rink and paused. He took a deep breath of the hockey rink air. "Ahhh! This is my happy place!" he said. He headed toward the locker room to get dressed.

Alex got out his gear and put on his shoulder pads first. Next, he put on his knee pads, then fastened his elbow pads in place. He put on his hockey socks next and pulled his breezers up over them. Alex threw on his lucky jersey that had, "Wisconsin" down the sleeve. Lastly, he put on his skates. Alex laced them up extra tight with a double knot. He tapped each skate three times. He did this just for good luck. Hockey players are superstitious. He grabbed his helmet and was about to head out to the rink when his lucky puck rolled out of his bag.

Hannah bent down to grab the puck. Holding it up she read out loud, "We'll miss you, Flash." She paused. "Who's Flash? Who signed this, Alex?"

Alex responded shyly, "Oh . . . all my teammates signed that after my last game in Wisconsin."

Hannah slowly smiled. "Oh . . . now we know what we can call you!" Hannah

said as she tossed the puck back to him. "The nickname suits you perfectly. You're the fastest one on the ice."

—

The coach blew the whistle from the center of the ice. The kids all skated out to the large red circle and took a knee.

"Alright, kids. Today is a tryout. All we ask is that you skate hard, do your best, and have fun!" the coach said smiling.

"We are going to start off by seeing how fast you can skate. We want to see your crossovers. Show us you can stop without running into the boards. We will take a quick water break. Finally, we will finish today's tryouts with passing and shooting drills and a little three-on-three." The coach blew the whistle again and the kids all lined up on the blue line.

Hannah lined up next to Alex and came to a quick stop. She sprayed ice all over him and smiled.

"Hey Flash!" she said. "You ready?"

"Get ready to eat my dust!" he replied, grinning.

The coach blew the whistle and Hannah and Alex took off with the other players. They pumped their arms and legs. Both came to an abrupt stop at the exact same time! They finished in front of the pack.

They were both huffing and puffing. They were out of breath but smiling.

"That was epic!" Alex said between breaths.

"No joke! I can see why they call you Flash!" Hannah replied.

The two kids were chatting about the next crossover drill and not paying any attention to the others finishing the stopping drill. All of a sudden, BAM! BOOM! SPLAT!

"Ahhhhhhhh!" Alex yelped as he toppled into the net.

"Ooooops," said a familiar voice. "My bad!"

Frankie stood up, staring at Alex in the net. He picked up his stick and skated back toward the coach.

Ugh. He's the worst, Alex thought as he picked up his stick. *What a cheap shot!* He got back with the other kids and continued to do the drills.

After awhile, the kids all took a break on the bench. They chugged water and caught their breaths. They were finishing up the last part of the day's tryout, so Alex tried to keep his distance from Frankie.

He wanted to show the coaches his skills. Alex wanted to show how great of a teammate he was. One of the reasons his teammates loved playing with him back home was because he passed the puck to them. Alex knew how to help his teammates score.

"Frankie, Alex, Hannah, and Rome," the coach yelled. "You're up next for some passing drills. Get on the line."

The players lined up side by side on the blue line. They placed their sticks down and got in the ready position. They looked back and forth at each other while squatting low and gripping their sticks.

The coach blew the whistle. The kids skated fast toward the net. Alex got the puck first. He passed it with ease straight to Hannah. She cradled the puck and passed it over to Rome.

Rome deked to the left. His fake-out was perfect. Then he passed it over to Frankie while the other three kept skating toward the goal. They were wide open, waiting for the puck.

"Pass!" Hannah yelled to Frankie.

"I'm open!" hollered Rome.

"Over here!" Alex shouted, tapping his stick on the ice.

Frankie ignored them and kept skating with the puck. He was trying to show off, but his skills said otherwise. He skated fast toward the goalie and refused to pass the puck. He wanted to be the one to score the goal.

He was skating full speed and pulled his stick back to shoot. He tried to stop but tripped. BAM! He went flying into the goal, taking the goalie with him. The only thing not in the net was the puck.

Frankie was lying on the ice, staring

at the rafters. He felt his face get red and hot. Frankie was embarrassed but didn't want to admit that to the other kids. He slowly got up and skated toward the bench to get a sip of water. He didn't even apologize to the goalie he had taken down.

"Hey, Frankie!" The coach hollered. "You need to learn to pass the puck if you want any playing time." The coach made some notes on his clipboard.

Frankie nodded to the coach. He slowly stood up and skated away with his head down. He looked defeated.

Alex overheard the coach talking to Frankie. He could tell Frankie felt bummed out, but Alex also knew that the coach was right. If Frankie did not learn to pass the puck, he'd hurt himself and the team.

As Hannah watched, she mumbled, "That's what you get for hogging the puck, ya big bully . . ."

Alex looked at Hannah and nodded silently in agreement.

But then he looked at Frankie again. Alex had been in his shoes before. He knew what it felt like to be disciplined in front of all the other players.

At that moment, Alex decided he wanted to help Frankie.

Alex skated toward the bench where Frankie was sitting. He slowed down right before he got to the boards. Alex leaned against the boards with his hip and propped his stick up next to him.

Alex took his mouthguard out and said, "Hey, Frankie. I'm heading over to the pond after school tomorrow if you want to pass the puck around."

Frankie looked stunned. He shot back, "Why would I want *your* help?"

Alex responded, "It's up to you if you make the team or not. I'll be at the pond with or without you. If you want help, I'll be there."

Frankie sat in silence for a minute. He finally said quietly, "Uh, we'll see," before standing up and skating off to join the rest of the group.

Alex knew Frankie wasn't going to be his best friend. That was for sure. But Alex knew how to be respectful and how to be a good teammate. If he helped Frankie learn how to pass, the team would be better for it.

The rest of the tryout was great. Hannah had a hat trick during the scrimmage and ran circles around everyone else. Rome and Alex made a few great shots and passes to each other. They all left the ice that day hopeful that the rest of the tryouts would be just as good.

CHAPTER 9

THE SHOOTOUT

AFTER ALEX GOT HOME FROM SCHOOL, he got ready to head to the pond. When he arrived, he was surprised to see Frankie already taking shots on the goal. He was by himself and seemed frustrated. Alex could hear him mumbling words to himself every time he shot the puck.

Alex walked up and dropped his hockey bag. He began to get his skates on. Frankie still didn't notice him sitting there. He cleared his throat to get his attention.

"Ahem!" Alex coughed loudly into his fist.

"Oh, hi," Frankie said. "I didn't see you sitting there."

"No problem. I didn't want to scare you." Alex said.

"I never get scared," Frankie snapped back.

"Are you sure about that?" Alex laughed. "You seemed pretty scared at tryouts when Coach told you to pass the puck."

Frankie stopped skating. He looked at Alex. First, he looked mad. Then slowly, a small smile started to peek out under his helmet.

"Ok, New Guy. So, you're a *funny guy* too, huh?" Frankie said. "Look. I wasn't scared when Coach called me out. I was mad more than anything."

Alex finished tying his skates. He stood up and skated up next to Frankie.

"Is making the top team important to you?" Alex asked Frankie.

"Of course!" Frankie replied.

"Then, I hate to break the news, man, but you need to listen to Coach on this one," Alex said, skating toward the net.

Frankie followed him. Alex started stick handling the puck. He moved it gracefully back and forth. Right before he got to the net, he stopped. Frankie was skating right behind Alex and headed toward the net. Alex made a back-handed pass to Frankie, who pulled his stick back and shot. GOAL!

"Nice One-Timer, Frankie!" Alex shouted. He smiled at Frankie.

Frankie looked shocked. He stood there staring at the puck in the goal. "Whoa! That was sick! I've never made one of those before!"

Alex skated toward Frankie and fist-bumped him.

"It's simple," Alex said. "You gotta have someone who knows how to pass." Alex snagged the puck out of the net and began to skate with it again.

"Remember, Frankie, if you look good, I look good too," Alex said.

"Huh?" Frankie skated toward Alex.

Alex continued. "When you pass the puck, you have to lead the puck to the player. Right when they are slightly ahead of you, look at your target and pass. Then it's all about the follow through." Alex showed him with his stick and the puck. He cradled the puck and then passed it back to Frankie.

Frankie cradled the puck and tried to pass it back to Alex. He fired it off into the side of the pond. It didn't go anywhere near Alex. It landed in a pile of grass and sticks. Alex passed him another puck from the stack on the ice and said, "Here, let's try that again."

This time when Frankie took his shot, he did what Alex said. He waited until Alex was just ahead of him. Frankie looked at his target and put the blade of his stick on the ice. He fired it back to Alex. Alex roofed it into the back of the net.

They skated toward each other and Frankie gave Alex a fist bump with his glove. Alex stared at his glove in disbelief.

"What are you looking at?" Frankie asked. "Come on, let's pass some more."

Alex kept staring at his glove.

"Wait . . . did Frankie Houser just thank me?" He looked up, smiling and laughing.

"Don't let it get to your head, Alex. Now come on. I need to pass a few

more of these before I see Coach this week."

The two kids stayed on the ice practicing passing drills. At one point, Alex looked up and spotted Blake standing next to his bike watching them from far away. Blake lifted his chin to Alex and smiled. A few minutes later, he got back on his bike and rode away.

Alex helped Frankie learn how to pass to a target. They were both shocked when Frankie started hitting his target every time. As the weather got colder and the sun went down, the boys called it a night and each headed home for dinner. Frankie learned that Alex was actually a nice kid. Most of all, he learned that Alex was a team player. The kids left with mutual respect for each other.

The next day at school, Blake stopped Alex on the way to the cafeteria.

"Hey, Alex. I saw you shooting pucks with Frankie yesterday," Blake said.

"Oh yeah. It was nothing really," Alex responded shyly. He stared at his feet.

"Well, I thought it was really cool of you to do, given that Frankie has been bullying you since you got here and all."

"Thanks, Blake," Alex said. "See you at the pond later?"

"You know it! Later, Flash," Blake said as he walked away.

The bell rang and Ms. Presley passed out the grades for the science experiment. Their group got a B+. Her notes said they needed to get better at working as a team. Ms. Presley handed out the next assignment to the group:

making crystals. All the students gathered around the table, staring at the materials. The group was more quiet than usual. They were waiting for Frankie to start bossing them around. Then he spoke.

"Hey, listen up," he said. "Turns out, the New Kid over here actually knows what he's talking about."

Frankie pointed his thumb at Alex. The group looked around at one other. They realized Frankie had had a change of heart. He wasn't going to be mean to Alex or start hogging the project. He was willing to participate in the group.

Alex stood up and grabbed the marker. Like in hockey, he started making the game plan for the science group. The kids leaned against the table and listened to Alex before they started. When he finished, he asked the group one more question.

"Hey, guys, what kind of dogs do scientists have?" Alex paused. "LABratory Retrievers! Get it?"

The kids burst out laughing.

"Whatever, Funny Guy." Frankie said, smiling. He rolled his eyes and said, "Let's go make some crystals."

CHAPTER 10

AT THE RINK, ALL THE KIDS STOOD outside the locker room. The roster was posted to the locker room door. They were crowded around, trying to look over each other's shoulders.

"Did you see it yet?" Hannah yelled toward Alex.

"No, I can't see it. Can you?" Alex replied.

"Yeah, but you're gonna want to see for yourself," she said.

Alex had a knot in his stomach. He made his way through the crowd of

kids. One by one they started walking away. He could finally see the list hanging on the gray clipboard. Because the list was in alphabetical order, his name was at the top. There it read, "Alex Alvarez" in bold letters. He did it! He made the top team—the A team.

Hannah and Frankie also made the team. They were all going to be teammates. Hopefully, now that Alex had squashed the bullying, they could learn how to play together better. They didn't have to be best friends, but they would need to learn how to work as a team.

"Hey, Alex!" Frankie called out. Alex was walking out of the rink. Frankie jogged to catch up to him. "Congrats! I saw that you made the A team!"

"Hey, thanks. Same to you!" Alex said.

They kept walking toward their parents' cars. Alex was about to get in when Frankie said, "Oh and hey . . .

thanks for the help the other day. If it weren't for the extra practice, I'm not sure I would have made the top team."

Alex gave him a quick nod. "No problem. That's what teammates are for, right?"

Alex got in the car. As soon as the door shut, his mom said, "Well . . . what team did you make?"

"I made the A team!" Alex shouted. He started doing a happy dance in the backseat. Connor started chanting, "A Team! A Team!" from his car seat. He danced around trying to copy his brother.

"Way to go, Alex! I knew you could do it! I hope you feel as proud of yourself as I am." His mom smiled in the rearview mirror.

She drove the boys to pick up a pizza on the way home. This called for a celebration.

CHAPTER 11

DREAMS COME TRUE

THE BELL RANG AND THE KIDS started to line up from recess. Alex was at the very back of the line with Hannah. Blake walked by and said, "Hannah, did you ask him yet?"

Alex looked confused. "Ask me what?" he said.

"To the Avalanche game! We have an extra ticket and my dad said we could take a friend. It's yours if you can come," Blake said smiling.

"They are playing the Knights on Friday," Hannah added. "It's going to be awesome."

"Seriously? No way!" Alex replied.

"Dead serious!" Hannah laughed. "Let me know tonight at practice if you can come, okay?"

Alex was so excited. He had never been to a real NHL game before. He only got to watch them on TV. This would be a dream come true! He hoped his mom and dad would allow him to go.

"I will ask the minute I get home from school!" Alex said. "Thanks!"

He couldn't wait for the dismissal bell to ring.

Alex's parents had met Blake and Hannah's parents during tryouts. They had also met briefly at the pond. Alex's parents felt comfortable with him going to the game.

—

Friday night, Alex was so excited he could hardly stand it. He threw his Av's jersey on over his hoodie and was ready to go. When Hannah rang the doorbell, Alex ripped the door open.

"Hey, Flash! You ready for this?" Hannah asked excitedly.

"Oh, I'm so ready! Let's go!" he said.

The kids ran to the car where Blake was waiting with his mom.

—

Alex walked into the arena. His mouth was agape in wonder. "Whoa!" he said, spinning around in a circle. "This is crazy cool!"

The arena was buzzing with excitement. There were fans walking to their seats, high-fiving strangers. The smell of hamburgers, hot dogs, and pizza floated through the air. Kids were

holding cotton candy and foam fingers, and dancing to the music playing on the loudspeakers. The massive Jumbotron TV screens hung above the center ice. TV screens were replaying highlights of the previous game. Nowhere else could you feel like you're on top of the action.

The kids made their way toward their seats. The man waiting to take their tickets stopped the kids and said, "Hey Hannah. Hey Blake! Good to see you two again!"

They smiled and Blake said, "You too, Tino! This is our friend Alex. It's his first NHL game!"

The man exchanged a funny look with Blake and Hannah. He said, "Oh! Then this will be a good surprise." He winked at the kids.

The kids started walking toward their seats.

"What was that about?" Alex asked curiously.

"You'll see . . . C'mon. We want to be there for the puck drop," Hannah said smiling.

Alex shrugged his shoulders and kept walking. The kids walked past a bunch of people and rows. They kept walking down the staircase. Alex thought to himself, *Where in the world are these seats?* The kids kept getting closer and closer to the ice.

Finally, Blake stopped at the first row. He pointed to their seats.

"Here we are!" he said.

The seats were in the front row! Alex couldn't believe it! Not only did he get to be at a game but he had seats right on the glass! This was every hockey fan's dream come true.

"NO WAY!" Alex shouted.

"Oh, yes-way!" Hannah said.

Alex asked, "Who is this seat for? There is one for me, Blake, you, and your mom. But this one is empty."

A deep voice chimed in, "There you are!" Hannah turned and gave the man a giant hug.

"Daddy!" Hannah said, squeezing the man tight.

Alex froze. His mouth opened and his jaw just about hit the floor.

"Wait! You . . ." Alex said, staring at the man. He looked back at Hannah and then at Blake.

"You know J-j-joe Cr-crosby?" he stuttered.

His throat felt dry. His eyes were probably bugging out of his head. He suddenly felt like he might pee his pants or pass out—he wasn't sure which.

"Know him?" Hannah said giggling. "Uh, yeah . . . he's my dad."

"Wait a minute . . . your dad is Joe? THEE Joe Crosby? As in . . . one of the greatest defensemen of all time?"

"Well until one of these young kids beats my record someday... but yeah, I guess that's me." Joe held out his hand to shake Alex's. "Nice to meet you, Alex!"

Alex could not believe that he was shaking his hero's hand. He almost forgot to let go!

"We were going to tell you on the pond," Blake said smiling. "Then we thought it'd be more fun to surprise you."

"Uh . . . best surprise ever!" Alex said. He stood there in shock.

"We're really glad you moved here, Alex," Hannah said.

"Yeah, you're not so bad," Blake said smiling. "And it was pretty cool to see how you treated Frankie. Especially

since he was being a Fartknocker to all you guys."

"Oh, it was nothing." Alex said.

"Yes, it was something," Hannah replied. "You stood up for us. You were a good friend to the group. And you were even a nicer person to help Frankie during tryouts."

"Eh, I just try to treat people how I'd like to be treated," Alex shrugged.

"Ladies and gentlemen..." the announcer said over the loudspeaker. The game was about to start. The kids turned their attention toward the ice. Smoke billowed out of the player's tunnel. Music played and the fans stood on their feet and cheered. One by one the players came out of the tunnel and started skating in a circle.

"You ready for this?" Mr. Crosby leaned down to ask Alex.

"So ready!" Alex replied.

"Looks to me like good things happen to good people," Joe said.

Finally, the puck dropped and the game started. The team had some jump in their legs tonight. The Avs scored a goal in the first minute of the game! The crowd went wild!

The game was as good as they get. Both the Avs and the Knights played great. Each team scored before the end of the second period. By the time the buzzer went off at the end of the third period, the game was tied, 2-2.

"I cannot wait to video chat Will when I get home. He's not going to believe this!" Alex said to Hannah.

"Isn't this awesome?" Blake shouted to Alex over the noisy crowd.

"You mean watching the game go into overtime while standing next to my friends and my hockey HERO?" he said. "Uhhh . . . YES!"

Joe grabbed his ticket out of his back pocket. He scribbled something on it with a pen and handed it to Alex.

"Wait . . . did you just . . . " Alex stammered. He stared at the hockey legend's autograph he was holding in his hand.

"It's all yours, kid!" Joe said, smiling.

"BEST. DAY. EVER!" he shouted, jumping up and down. He was so excited he hugged Joe and then pulled away. "I mean, uh cool, Mr. Crosby. Uh . . . thanks for the autograph!"

"Just call me Joe," he replied. "Hannah, Blake, and I are headed to the pond for an early skate tomorrow. You want to come?"

Alex grinned ear to ear. "Oh Joe, I need to check my schedule," he paused. "Yup! I'm free!" he said immediately.

The kids started laughing.

"Dad, everyone calls Alex "Flash"

because he's the fastest kid on the ice!" Blake said.

"Yeah, he's hard to catch," Hannah continued. "And get this! He stood up to this bully at school during our science experiment! He totally helped our group."

The kids were talking a mile a minute. "Yeah, he even helped the kid learn how to pass," Blake added. "Without Alex, he wouldn't have made the team."

Alex stood there looking back and forth at his friends as they talked. His cheeks started to turn pink.

Joe looked at the kids with a big smile on his face. "Alex, it sounds like you are the type of friend everyone wants to have. It pays to be a good teammate, Alex. You just never know who you'll meet," he winked.

The game went into overtime. The fans were on the edges of their seats. It was intense. Every pass, steal, and breakaway had fans screaming and cheering. The Avs team captain got the puck and skated fast down the ice toward the goal. Suddenly, he made a backward pass to the winger. It was a hard pass to pick up unless it was perfect. His teammate cradled the puck and shot it right in between the goalie's legs! GOALLLLLLL!

The fans went crazy! The kids jumped up and down and high-fived everyone sitting near them. The Avs won the game 3-2. It was a game Alex would remember forever.

They all filed out of the stadium talking about the perfect pass that won the game.

Alex looked up at the mountain skyline and smiled. When he first moved to this new city, he had no idea what it would be like. But at that moment, he knew he was *exactly* where he was supposed to be.

ABOUT THE AUTHOR

Meghan Hertzfeldt is an author of twin pregnancy preparation books and now venturing into sports fiction children's lit. She constantly generates ideas for books at the hockey rink, ball field, or courts. For years, Meghan dreamed of writing children's books the way she thought they should be written: entertaining humorous stories with unique plots that are based on character-building traits and integrity.

Meghan loves to play goalie in the basement while her twin boys shoot pucks at her face. She is a pickleball enthusiast, has climbed a "14er" in Colorado, and has outrun wild boars on a beach in Mexico.

 www.gametimetheseries.com

 @gametimetheseries

 https://www.facebook.com/gametimetheseries

ABOUT THE ILLUSTRATOR

Lindsay Leal is not only a children's illustrator, she's got other talents as well. She used to work in digital advertising when she realized she loved two things: summer camp (where she met Meghan) and her time at boarding school. She moved to Connecticut to pursue a career in education. Now she lives on campus at a boarding school with her dog, Scout, where she works in the Dean's office and teaches math. In addition to coaching field hockey, Lindsay loves needlepoint projects, reruns of 80s and 90s sitcoms, and wandering around fancy grocery stores.